MIND**BREAKING**

What the World Won't Tell You about Forgiveness

Naomi Cornelius

BK
ROYSTON
Publishing

Cover Layout: Elite Covers
Cover Image: Rev. Faith Cole

Editing and Interior Layout: BK Royston Publishing LLC
ISBN-13: 978-1-946111-98-2

Printed in the United States of America

WITH GRATITUDE

I humbly give thanks to my Heavenly Father, my Lord and Savior Jesus Christ, my entire family, church family, and friends.

I thank those who have contributed to my life that are not in those categories.

I pray that God will continue to bless us all in every endeavor that is in His Will, and may we continue to bask in His blessings and chase after Him. He is the everlasting fountain that never runs dry.

Table of Contents

Introduction

"Let us lay aside every weight, and the sin which so easily ensnares us." Hebrews 12:1b

Refusing to forgive causes a heavy load, because it weighs a person down spiritually, mentally, and physically. He/she may not realize that an unforgiving spirit is slowing them down and hindering their purpose, plan, and progress. One becomes locked up like a prisoner, and the one with the key that has him/her in bondage is the very one that they have a problem with forgiving. The reason why they have the key is because they have gone on about their daily routine, and the one in bondage refuses to forgive and maybe contemplating revenge. For example, in a chess game, instead of you taking the initiative to move and strategize, you allow the one with the key to strategize and make you move based on their move. Your opponent sees where you're going on the board, but because you won't forgive or reconcile, you are blinded by what they are doing on the board. You become trapped, and your opponent says, "*Checkmate*!" Before getting trapped, it behooves you to forgive, release , and ask God to give you the strength to go through. Then you will have the right key to unlock your cell and set yourself free.

In the game of monopoly, a player can buy, sell, or trade property. He/she can easily be placed in jail and have to stay in jail or choose to buy their way out of jail. It seems easier to keep a "Get out of jail" card or cash on hand or else the player would have to give up houses and property.

LET GO and LET GOD

I.   Let go and let God (***Cast your cares on Him***). It is much healthier; it eliminates so much stress and worry.

II.   We wrestle with the old and the new self. So why put yourself in the frontline on the battlefield of the mind. Unforgiving robs one of his/her ammunition.

III.   Release by restoring your mind.

IV.   Having peace of mind strengthens us, and it comes from God.

V.   Life is a stage. The mind is a platform (negative or positive). Everything that is done, it is ***thought*** of first in the mind.

VI.   Don't play the Blame Game with God.

Less Weight on the Brain: "I have learned to

forgive."

NOTES/REFLECTION

_____

_____

_____

_____

_____

_____

_____

_____

_____

_____

_____

_____

_____

_____

_____

_____

NOTES/REFLECTION

_____

_____

_____

_____

_____

_____

_____

_____

_____

_____

_____

_____

_____

_____

_____

_____

PURPOSE LIVING

I.   What is your purpose?

II.   God's plan for your life

"I am a working progress"

Some people don't have any idea of you being mad at them, so you are really mad with yourself.

We have been……

1. Lied to

2. Set up

3. Misused

4. Abused

5. The other woman.

6. The other man

NOTES/REFLECTION

_____

_____

_____

_____

_____

_____

_____

_____

_____

_____

_____

_____

_____

_____

_____

_____

_____

_____

LOVE

John 3:16

John 15:12

What is Love?	I Corinthians 13:4-7
Love your neighbors	Leviticus 19:18
Love covers all sins	Proverbs 10:12
Love your enemies	Matthew 5:44
Love never fails	I Corinthians 13:8
No fear in love	I John 4:18,19

NOTES/REFLECTION

_____

_____

_____

_____

_____

_____

_____

_____

_____

_____

_____

_____

_____

_____

_____

_____

_____

FORGIVING IS A PROCESS

A process is a series of actions or operations directed towards a particular result. Some of the steps towards forgiving are as follows:

1. Deny Self

2. Try not to wait for a sickbed or deathbed scenario to occur for a platform to list your regrets and to give your apologies

3. Do not become the devil's advocate

4. Get rid of dead weight

5. Reverse your circumstances in dry places

Lack of resources, Lack of water

Thirsty (What are you thirsty for today?)

A dry place is where you are occupying space, but you are not moving forward. There is no growth, no elevation, no great expectations, no sunshine, no milestones, no water...

I have sat in the seat of dry places, and it was imperative that I stood up and made a change. Examples of dry places are the act of abusing others and being abused, refusing to forgive but wanting other to apologize to you, refusing to exercise the gift God gave you, or dating someone's wife or husband.

In most cases, true friends fall out with each other, but they eventually forgive one another. Forgetting is not forgiving. Refusing to forgive can have a domino effect.

Some people are still angry over something that happened over thirty years ago. A thief is mad at another thief for stealing.

FORGIVING DEFERRED

1. Forfeit some of your blessings

2. Overlook your benefits for being obedient

3. Reduce your faith

4. Grief

5. Ignores the Holy Spirit

6. Victimize Self

7. Eventually becomes bitter

Remember...

To forge a relationship is to imitate with the intent to defraud

One commits infringement if he/she tries to act as if he/she is the producer of grace.

Popular questions and statements

I can forgive, but I cannot forget

Is forgiving forgetting?

Why bad things happen to good people?

Why should I apologize? I didn't do anything.

Why do I still feel hurt after all these years?

Where was God?

FORGIVING IS NOT FORGETTING

What is Forgiving?

1.

2.

3.

4.

5.

MINDBREAKING THE PROMISE

What is the Promise God gave to us about forgiving?

1. _____

2. _____

3. _____

4. _____

5. _____

6. _____

7. _____

8. _____

9. _____

10.   _____

MINDBREAKING

THE PIECES OF THE PUZZLE

What pieces (words) of a forgiveness puzzle would you put together?

A.

_____

_____

B.

_____

_____

C.

_____

_____

D.

_____

_____

E.

_____

_____

F.

_____

_____

FORGIVENESS IS THE KEY TO ACTION AND FREEDOM

1. You are no longer a participant of a generational curse

2. A curse is something that is cursed (Evil or Misfortune)

3. Putting away the past

4. Generational holdbacks (Inheritance, habits, negative phrases…)

5. Scared to tell about past misfortunes

6. Fearful of revisiting the past (It can be painful)

7. Wasteful relationships

8. Debt (Not only financially)

9. Being proactive, making it right, and living in your liberty

10. What is a blessing?

Study Lesson: _David and Mephibosheth_

2 Samuel 9:1-13

THE QUESTION (Key Verse)

Is there yet any that is left of the house of Saul, that I may shew him kindness for Jonathan's sake? (NKJV)

"David asked, "Is there anyone still left in the house of Saul to whom I can show kindness for Jonathan's sake?"

(NIV Prophecy Study Bible)

Terms/People

David

Saul

Jonathan

Ziba

Makir

Lo Debar

Ammiel

Mephibosheth

Micah

Restored

Crippled

Summoned

Reference Scriptures

2 Samuel 9:1 **(1 Samuel 20:14-17, 42)**

2 Samuel 9:2 **(2 Samuel 16:1-4, 19:17, 26,29)**

2 Samuel 9:3 **(1 Samuel 20:14)**

2 Samuel 9:4 **(2 Samuel 17:27-29)**

2 Samuel 9:6 **(Genesis 37:7)**

2 Samuel 9:7 **(2 Samuel 19:28)**

2 Samuel 9:8 **(2 Samuel 4:4, 3:8)**

2 Samuel 9:10 **(2 Samuel 16:3)**

2 Samuel 9:11 **(Job 36:7/Psalms 113:8)**

2 Samuel 9:12 **(2 Samuel 4:4)**

NOTES/REFLECTION

_____

_____

_____

_____

_____

_____

_____

_____

_____

_____

_____

_____

_____

_____

_____

_____

_____

SUMMARY

Most kings in David's day tried to wipe out the families of their rivals in order to prevent any descendants from seeking the throne. David showed kindness to Mephibosheth, whose father was Jonathan and whose grandfather was King Saul. David was king. Partly because of his loyalty to God's previously anointed king and partly for political reasons to unite Judah and Israel. But more importantly, because of his vow to show kindness to all of Jonathan's descendants. How Mephibosheth became crippled is recorded in 2 **Samuel 4:4**. Mephibosheth was five years old when Saul and Jonathan died and when the nurse ran with him, she dropped him in her haste. He became lame in both feet.

Mephibosheth was afraid to visit King David, who wanted to treat him like a prince. Although Mephibosheth **feared for his life,** and may have felt unworthy, that didn't mean he should refuse David's gifts. **When God graciously offers us forgiveness of sins and a place in heaven**, we may feel unworthy, but we will receive these gifts if we accept them. A reception even warmer than the one David gave Mephibosheth awaits all who receive God's gifts through trusting Jesus Christ; not because we deserve it, but because of God's promise **(Ephesians 2:8-9)**

David's treatment of Mephibosheth shows **his integrity as a leader** who accepted his obligation **to show love and mercy.** His generous provision for Jonathan's son goes beyond any political benefit he might have received. **Are you able to forgive those who have wronged you? Can you be generous with those less deserving?**

Each time we show compassion, our character is strengthened.

THE PRODIGAL SON

PORTION

PROMISCUOUS LIVING

PENNILESS PLIGHT

PRIDE DEFERRED

PAPA'S PREPARATION

PARTY TIME

12 Twelve Things that can Happen Because of an Unforgiving Attitude

1. Fall **out** of fellowship with God

2. Allow Satan to **Stagnate** my growth

3. Self-Infliction (**chained up**)

4. Build **Barriers**

5. Mixed messages surface (**confusion**)

6. Loaded **down** with baggage

7. Holiness lifestyle is **hindered**

8. **Forfeit** God's Favor

9. **Enemy** towards Self

10. **Blocked** Blessings

11. Comfortable in **Bondage**

12. **Effects** relationships

CPPR GRAPH

Challenges	**Process**
Possibilities	**Results**

NOTES/REFLECTION

_____

_____

_____

_____

_____

_____

_____

_____

_____

_____

_____

_____

_____

_____

_____

_____

_____

_____

Grace Period I

I believe a grace period isn't just a time of mercy given to someone who needs to pay a bill. I believe it is a continual period issued by God, whether we deserve it or not. A Grace Period is extended days, weeks, months or even years given for us to utilize. It is up to us to acknowledge what we have and use it to our advantage. Nevertheless, some people choose to ignore the mere fact that extended time is given for us to get it right with God and our fellowman.

There was a man who was selling all his possessions. The reason he gave was because he wanted to go to see his family and make things right. He said, "I need to go get it right with my family and friends and ask them and God for forgiveness." He was so anxious and, in a hurry, that I thought someone was after him.

It seems as if he could not leave quick enough. So, I asked him was he sick? He responded with a yes. He told me that he was very sick and didn't have long to live. I asked him for his name and told him that I would be praying for him. Later, it dawned on me that I should have prayed for him right then. It was the appropriate thing to do. He started to tell me about what all he had materially. He begins to curse and brag about how tough of a guy he had been back in the day. I started to think that maybe this man is drunk. At the end of our conversation, I begin to realize that he had been drinking, but he was so honest about forgiving. He said he wanted to see his family and say his goodbyes. A lot of people refuse to say goodbye, even on the phone. Saying goodbye, is not a likable word. Regardless of how drunk this man might have been, he was sincere in letting someone know that he was sorry. I believe if the man never did reach his family to ask for forgiveness, that in his heart, he was forgiven, because he was trying to reconcile. On the other hand, he could call them on the phone, but that was not good enough. This man seemed to be real, and the bottom line was, he wanted to see their faces. He was making preparation for something to come. He did not go into detail other than, he expressed that he had undergone several operations, and he was tired. Surgery was not an option for him and he was finished with that. He looked tired, and yet he expressed how bad of a guy he was. Here was a man who did not know me from Jack or Jill, and yet he confided in me. Both of us were waiting for the same mechanic to work on our cars, and in our conversation, he was trying to sell me one of his cars.

I was reading this article, and the main

points I received from it was *challenges*, *possibilities*, *process*, and *results*. I call it the CPPR. When I look at this experience I had with this man who was making preparation to exit from this life, I don't know if he ever made it out-of-town. I am determined to ask the mechanic about him. I found out later that the mechanic is his brother.

Challenges

One of the challenges that he faced is trying to sell all that he has so he can travel and get things right with the people he has hurt. He is not trying to sell all that he has and give it to the poor, nor is he trying to build bigger barns. From my understanding, he has done many people wrong, and before the ***curtain of life*** closes on him, he wants to repent. Life is a challenge, and there are various challenges that we encounter daily.

There is nothing too hard for God. The nothing includes challenges. God will give us courage and strength to conquer the challenges.

Possibilities

One of the possibilities of this man situation is he may sell all his belongings, now what he does with the money remains to be seen. He expressed to me that it was too far to travel so he did not want to drive, and he did not want to carry a load. Another possibility is his **plans may be prolonged** if he does not sell his possessions in a timely matter. Another possibility is surrendering all to God, and let God direct his path. ***There is nothing impossible for God***.

Process

This man had a plan which was to sell all he had

and use the money to travel. One of the vehicles he wanted to sell me was a crown Victoria. It was a late model with dark tinted windows that looked like a cop car. I waited to test drive it, because I wanted my brother to be with me. He gave me the keys and he said start it up. The car did not start on the first try. He said hold on. He got in the car and did something special, and the car started up. Now, *the process changes.* Let's keep it real with cars. The car owner knows his/her car better than anyone, because it belongs to them. When the owner drives the car, and the car begins to act up, the owner knows exactly what to do without looking in the *manual.* Not to say the manual is not significant, because it is. It is a roadmap for instructions of how to operate and maintain the vehicle. God gives us the greatest book ever written, the Bible. It is a roadmap for life on how to know God, and how to exemplify a Christ-like life. The bible gives instructions on relationships with our heavenly Father, family, and mankind.

Results

As I mentioned earlier, the result remains to be seen. The man's intentions were to be with his family and friends. He was trying for that to be the end result. I can only hope that he made it to his planned destination. When I look at this whole scenario, I remembered the man's brother was the mechanic. The man was around family, but he was anxious to change locations, and see his other family members. Overall, his anticipation was to be around other loved ones, before his *expiration date*. Thank God the end result ends with Him.

NOTES/REFLECTION

_____

_____

_____

_____

_____

_____

_____

_____

_____

_____

_____

_____

_____

_____

_____

_____

_____

Grace Period II

I thank God for His grace. After experiencing an abusive relationship, the next relationship I encountered, the person I was involved with inherited my baggage. He had his own baggage, so why would I want to intrude on his life and make him miserable? Obviously, my baggage was too much for him. He was overloaded with baggage. I didn't care because I was wounded and miserable. I tried to be loving and kind because that was my personality. I didn't have patience anymore. I would fly off the handle at the tip of a hat. I think that's how that goes. Well, anyway, my guards were up and I had lost the passion of having a loving relationship.

Several years have passed and I still suffer from not being able to see him to let him know I was sorry. It was painful. I can attest to this, because when I was ashamed and sorry, I did not know how to contact him to reconcile. Many times, I would pray and wish I could see him. His face kept flashing in my mind and I knew it was sign. *I was reaping what I had sown*. That time finally came. We ran into each other and decided to call one another. We were able to talk and I was able to apologize to him. Even though my actions came from my abuse, I knew I had become a very angry person. This loving guy that I met did not deserve how I was treating him. I believe God placed him in my life, because he was a gentleman. He was kind, soft-spoken, he had a gorgeous smile and he was a Christian man. He had a lot of patience. I would be hollering and yelling at him for not speaking up when people tried to misuse him. Sometimes I would try to fuss about stuff on purpose. All along it was me. I was letting my past dictate my future. I thank God He allowed me to ask my friend to forgive me. *It is never too late to forgive, but remember, tomorrow isn't promised.*

NOTES/REFLECTION

_____

_____

_____

_____

_____

_____

_____

_____

_____

_____

_____

_____

_____

_____

_____

_____

HEAVEN'S HANDS

Whatever your will, I'll love you still,
You justified me,
I can testify,
You held back the hands of the enemy,
And delivered me.

You worked miracles,
I'm your child,
Like the children of the circle
Touched by heaven's hands. (2x)

Your unfailing love, Covers us all,
Your blood was shed,
For us all,
Thank you, Lord,
For I am touched by heaven's hands.

You have dried my tears,
In the late hours of the night,
You've woke me from my sleep,
To tell me,
Everything is going to be alright.

Now, I feel like going on,
You have made me strong.
Thank you, Lord,
For I am touched by heaven's hands.

I can go that extra mile,
I am your friend,
I have learned to smile again,
Thank you for the thunder,
Storms and rain in my life,
I can see sunlight once again.

Naomi Cornelius

JESUS and FORGIVENESS

Jesus forgave ...

The people who crucified Him.

The criminal on the cross.

Peter, for denying he knew Jesus.

The woman who anointed His feet with oil.

The woman caught in adultery.

The paralytic lowered on a mat through the roof

1. In order to be lifted, you must be lowered
2. Whose house were they in?
3. The condition, the crowd,
4. A divine distraction
5. A devastating condition

Jesus saw their faith!

Loose those chains by forgiving, and asking for forgiveness.

CHAINS of GUILT

CHAINS of PEER PRESSURE

CHAINS of LOW SELF ESTEEM

CHAINS of "IF I ONLY HAD....NO, LET IT GO MOVEFORWARD

CHAINS of ABUSE (IT'S MY FAULT), NO.... STOP TAKING UP FOR THE PERSON THAT KEEPS BEATING ON YOU. WE WERE NOT MEANT TO BE DOOR MATS OR PUNCHING BAGS.

You can forgive the abuser, but don't keep stepping in the same mud because it gets muddier, and muddier. You want to guard your temple, because your body is the temple of God.

God has purposed a great life for you.

"For I know the thoughts that I think towards you, says the Lord, thoughts of peace and not of evil, to give you a future, and a hope." (Jeremiah 29:11) NKJV

Love Renewed in Lebanon

Song of Solomon 8: 6-7

"Set me as a seal upon thine **heart**, as a seal upon thine **arm**; for **love** is strong as death; **jealousy** is cruel as the grave; the coals thereof are coals of fire, which hath a most **vehement flame**. Many waters cannot quench love, neither can the floods drown it; if a man would give all the **substance** of his house for love, it would utterly be contemned."

Lebanon lies at the eastern end of the Mediterranean Sea, north of Israel and west of Syria. It is four-fifths the size of Connecticut.

(Lebanon flag and Coat of Arms)

The capital and largest city in Beirut, and the official language is Arabic. Greater Lebanon was in the mandate of Syria. (Language- French), Religion- Christianity/Islam

The Power of Love

Love cannot be killed by time or disaster. It cannot be bought for any price, because it is freely given. Love is priceless. Even the richest king cannot buy it. Love must be accepted as a gift from God and then shared within the guidelines God provides. Accept the love of your spouse as God's gift and strive to make your love a reflection of the perfect love that comes from God himself.

Luke 7:42

King James Version

And when they had nothing to pay, he frankly

_____

them both.   Tell
me therefore, which of them will

_____him most?

Ephesians 4:32

And be ye_____one to
another,

_____,

forgiving one another, even as God for

_____   _____

hath forgiven you.

Colossians 3:13

_____

one another, and forgiving one another, if any man have a

_____

against any; even as Christ forgave you, so also do ye.

Psalm 86:5

For thou, Lord, art

_____

, and

_____

to forgive; and plenteous in

_____unto
_____them that call

upon thee.

Matthew 6:14

For if ye forgive men

their

_____, your

heavenly Father will also forgive you.

2 Corinthians 2:7

So that contrariwise ye ought rather to

forgive him, and

_____him,

lest perhaps such a one should be swallowed

up with overmuch_____.

I John 1:9

If we_____our
sins, he is

_____and just to
forgive us our sins, and to

_____

us from all

_____.

WORDS

Quarrel

Good

Ready

Mercy

All Forgave

Love

Kind

Tenderhearted

Trespasses

Comfort

Sorrow

Confess

Christ's sake

Forbearing

Faithful

Cleanse

Unrighteousness

NOTES/REFLECTION

_____

_____

_____

_____

_____

_____

_____

_____

_____

_____

_____

_____

_____

_____

_____

_____

MERCY

Mercy means a compassion or forbearance shown especially to an offender or to one subject to one's power; also, lenient or compassionate treatment; a blessing that is an act of divine favor or compassion. In **Hebrews 4:16** the Bible says, "Let us therefore come boldly unto the throne of grace that we may obtain mercy and find grace to help in time of need."

"Not by works of righteousness which we have done, but according to his mercy he saved us, by the washing of regeneration, and renewing of the Holy Ghost." **(Titus 3:5)**

"But God, who is rich in mercy, for his great love wherewith h loved us." **(Ephesians 2:4)**

"Therefore, seeing we have this ministry, as we have received mercy, we faint not."
(2 Corinthians 4:1)

Mercy begets Mercy **(Roman 11)**

"And His mercy is on them that fear him from generation to generation." **(Luke 1:50)**

"I will have mercy and not sacrifice, for I am not come to call the righteous, but sinners to repentance." **(Matthew 9:13b)**

"He hath shewed thee, O man, what is good; and what doth the Lord require of thee, but to do justly, and to love mercy, and to walk humbly with thy God? **(Micah 6:8)**

The Bible says," Let not mercy and truth forsake thee: bind them about thy neck; write them upon the table of thine heart; So shalt thou find favor and good understanding in the sight of God and man." **(Proverbs 3:3-4)**

"For the Lord is good; his mercy is everlasting; and his truth endureth to all generations."
(Psalm 100:5)

"Mercy and truth are met together; righteousness and peace have kissed each other." **(Psalms 85:10)**

"O give thanks unto the Lord; for he is good; for his mercy endureth forever." **(I Chronicles 16:34)**

(Numbers 14: 18a)

The Lord is longsuffering, and of great mercy forgiving iniquity and transgression.

Forgiveness…. Mercy……. Grace

NOTES/REFLECTION

_____

_____

_____

_____

_____

_____

_____

_____

_____

_____

_____

_____

_____

_____

_____

_____

Praying for my Enemies

I thank God for **His unconditional, unfailing love**. I Thank God for our love ones and people who care and demonstrate love for us through their actions. Love is an action word.

It's good to have friends, and it is good knowing who your enemies are. Surely, we won't know all our enemies, but we can identify some of them.

One day, I decided to pray for one of my enemies. I prayed and I cried. In the **process** of that heavy burden being lifted, I felt the Lord take a load of weight off my shoulder. I was delivered from what was keeping me in bondage. I was able to move **forward.**

Guess who was keeping me in bondage? Me.

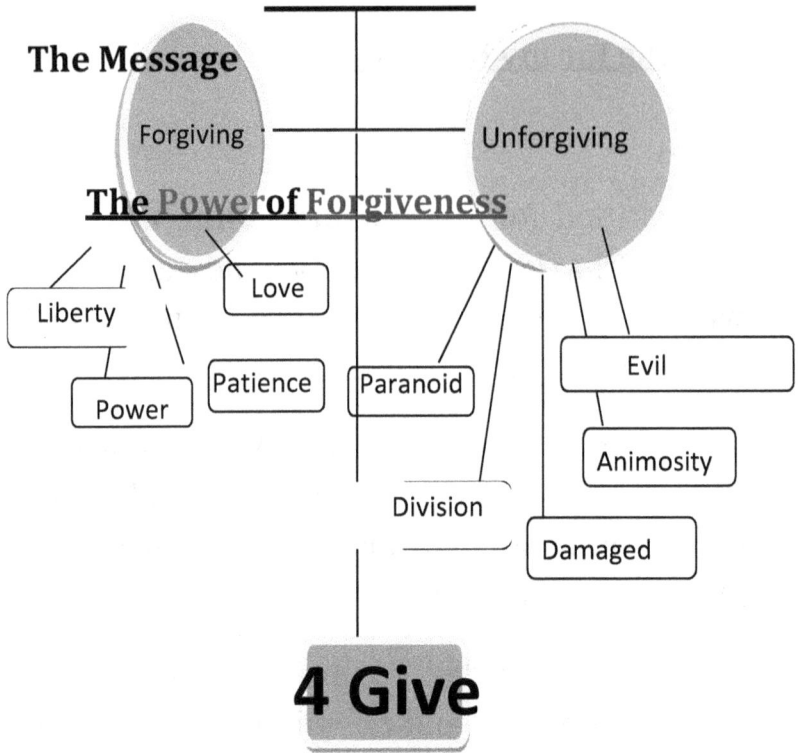

The Message

Forgiving — Unforgiving

The Power of Forgiveness

- Liberty
- Love
- Power
- Patience

- Paranoid
- Evil
- Animosity
- Division
- Damaged

4 Give

R

Reconcile

Revives

Restores

Rejuvenates

Retreats

Walking with the Enemy

Little did I know that on this day I would have to walk with my enemy. Coming out an event in South Dallas, I happened to look up and low and behold, one of my worst enemies is standing by me. This person was scared to walk to her vehicle, because of the neighborhood. By me being the person that I am, I volunteered to walk her to her car. I waited for the person to get in the car, lock up and drive off.

While we were walking to the car, we had very little dialogue. However, memories were passing through my mind. I just assumed since several years had passed and I have not heard, "I'm sorry," that maybe this is a way of the person saying, "Will you forgive me." It didn't happen. Maybe this was a *silent apology*. Some people cannot build enough courage to say I'm sorry; therefore, they will try and do some good deed for you to dismiss the pain they have caused you. My actions showed that I was saying I accept your apology even though your apology was nonverbal.

M.I.S.S

Make It Simple Saints

Forgiveness is for us to give and receive. To the unbelievers in Christ, Jesus Christ is the answer for the world today; so, it is imperative that we forgive for the sake of all mankind. I pray that every reader of this book has been introduced to the greatest gift that has been given to us, with mercy, grace and unconditional love in mind. II Chronicles 7:14 and Matthew 6:14 are essential to our daily lives, especially to the Christian's journey. The Bible says, "If my people who are called by my name will humble themselves, and pray and seek my face, and turn from their wicked ways, then I will hear from heaven, and will forgive their sin and heal their land" (II Chronicles 7:14). The Bible says, "For if you forgive men their trespasses, your heavenly Father will also forgive you" (Matthew 6:14, NKJV).

The more we forgive, we allow ourselves to invite reconciliation, restoration, and regeneration into our lives. When we refuse to forgive, we give Satan a thumbs-up and allow him to lead us in dangerous passage. I take full responsibility for sharing this information with you because I believe liberty is at the doorsteps of your heart. Your heart can be connected to God who authorizes forgiveness. There is no special strategy or chemistry of how this process works, but I know if you have a willing heart to forgive, you can work it. Some of the ingredients for this recipe is praying, trusting God, studying His Word, and moving forward through your faith. Release your Faith to Forgive, and Freedom is at your Fingertips!

NOTES/REFLECTION

_____

_____

_____

_____

_____

_____

_____

_____

_____

_____

_____

_____

_____

_____

_____

_____

What The World

Won't Tell You

About

FORGIVENESS

Naomi Cornelius

www.ingramcontent.com/pod-product-compliance
Lightning Source LLC
Chambersburg PA
CBHW052106270326
41931CB00012B/2906